EMILY LEARNS TO PRAY

Daniel B Lancaster & Jeffrey Lancaster
Illustrated by Cindy Monroy & Sarah Hernández

FOR RHYS

Every night Emily and her mama snuggled in bed
As she listened to the bedtime stories she read.

When she finished, they held hands as she prayed
Thanking God for Emily and all she learned that day.

One night, Emily said, "I want to learn to pray,
But I don't know how or what to say!"

Her mama smiled and said, "I'll teach you, Emily.
This is how your Grandma prayed with me."

To start we lift our hands in **PRAISE**
And give thanks for every new day.

We lift our hands to worship God
Because He's the one that made us all.

We praise God for the world He made
And for His peace when we feel afraid.

We thank Him for our family and friends
And for His blessings that never end.

Then, we make things **RIGHT** with God
And tell Him the times that we've done wrong.

We shape our hands into a heart
Because God gives us a brand-new start.

Just like how I wash your messy clothes

God makes your heart as white as snow.

ASKing God for help is the next part of prayer.
We know He loves us and really cares.

We hold out both hands to receive
Because it honors God when we believe.

We ask God to meet the needs of the world

And comfort hurting boys and girls.

We end our prayer by saying **YES**
To whatever God says 'cause He knows best.

Hold up your hands like you're honoring a king
'cause God is the ruler over everything.

God is with you wherever you go.
His plans for us are better than we know!

Jesus prayed like this in the garden,
"Your will, not mind, Heavenly Father."

Here's an easy way to remember each step
They spell **PRAY** - that's hard to forget!

P Is for **PRAISE** ...
Thank God for what He's done.

R Is for **RIGHT** ...
Tell God what you've done wrong.

A Is for **ASK** ...
Ask God for what we need.

Y Is for **YES** ...
We follow God wherever He leads.

Just like when you learned to ride your bike
Your prayers will get better the more you try.

You can always ask me if you need help
But soon you'll find what works best for yourself!

"Thanks Mama!" Emily said, "I'm ready to try!"
Then she said a prayer for the very first time.

THANKS FOR READING MY BOOK!

IF YOU ENJOYED IT PLEASE LEAVE A REVIEW ON AMAZON
SO MORE KIDS CAN FIND IT AND LEARN HOW TO PRAY.

go.lightkeeperbooks.com/emilyprays

JOIN MY LIGHTKEEPER KIDS CLUB TO RECIEVE A PDF WITH
COLORING PAGES AND MORE TIPS ON HOW TO PRAY!

ASK AN ADULT TO SIGN YOU UP AT:

go.lightkeeperbooks.com/kidsclub